D1482322

Anthology of Hope

GLASSSPIDERPUBLISHING

Edited by Vince Font
Cover design by Jane Font
Published by Glass Spider Publishing
www.glassspiderpublishing.com

To those who shoulder the burden when no one else will . . . and who will continue to do so for as long as it takes. Thank you.

Contents

Publisher's Note

The story of how this book came to be is a simple one. It came about because I needed it. Amid the dark and dismal days of late 2020 and early 2021, I found myself at an emotional and psychological nadir, searching anywhere I could from the safety of my home for confirmation that the spark of human decency—of compassion for the weak, of humanity toward the oppressed, and whispered kindnesses amid a nationwide scream fest—was still alive. I found that proof in words. Those words, along with the names of the individuals who wrote them, are contained within this book. I thank them all for showing me that hope can still exist, even in the bleakest of times—and for reminding me that all we have to do to exterminate the darkness is to call upon those carrying the light.

–Vince Font

The Tree

Vince Font

The tree outside my window
has withstood more than I.
It's no small wonder why:
Its roots are deep, and rooted to the earth—the
tree knows where it stands and wants nothing to
do with anyplace but here.
And when the torrents blow and the gales roll
in, its branches are yielding, swaying with the
current.
Sometimes it loses a limb.
But in these times it does not cry, or grieve for
its discarded parts.
It just goes on, standing tall, growing strong.
I wish I were the tree.

Te jkuxineltike

Yuria Celidwen

(Original Maya Tzeltal)

Te jkuxineltik ya ka'ytike
sok te ya jcholtike
ya jaltik te jkuxlejaltike.
Xtilnax te sejk'uite ek'etik
suto ik'alel xi'wel sok ipal k'ajk'aliletik
spisil jalbil te jich k'anbil, ta kuxineletik.
Jtsakojbajtik sok yantik,
ya jpasbajtik li' ta balumilal
sok te jkuxineltike . . .

~*~

Our Stories

Yuria Celidwen

(English translation)

From the stories we hear
and that we tell,
we weave our world.
From the intention of the star
to the chills of wind and the lightning's wrath,
we weave our land with stories.
Nourished by and bound with others,
we *become* the world
through stories . . .

Lullaby for the Weary Grown

C.W. Allen

Once upon a time
(when you were newer and wiser)
you called out in the dark
for Someone.

You needed to know
that Someone was there
padding slippered feet across the hall,
crouching low to the bed just your size.

The whisper you craved was not
It's only a dream
but
I am here.
You needed to know—
not that your fears were small and false,
but big enough
real enough
to matter.
Imaginary monsters cannot be beaten;
they live on in the dark corners of pretend

and grow big in the small hours.
Real things
have size, shape, weight;
they throw shadows in the light
that stretch and shrink with the sun's daily
dance.

Real things can be stuffed in pockets
torn in pieces
frayed at the edges
poked at the seams
studied with a smudged, borrowed detective's
glass,
their rough places rubbed smooth with
persistent fingertips
tested to see if they float or sink
or bounce or shatter,
broken into the blocks that made them up
so you can build them into something else
that suits you better.

Your newness has lost its polish;
the monsters under your bed
and the storm outside your window
have found their way inside.

You say you are Grown,
but
the things that are only made real by pretending
do not spook you like the things you pretended
too hard
were not monsters at all,
and would not test you
to see if you will float
or sink
or bounce or shatter.

So listen, child
(for we are all children at night):
the things that whisper to you in the dark are
too real
to be kicked under the bed
or buried with the smelly socks.
The tragedy of growing up
is that now you must be your own Someone
but
I am here,
your ghost of midnights past,
if you are not too Grown
to bend your ear for whispered secrets.

So sleep now, child.
What is real enough for midnight is real enough
for morning
when we have light enough to see its face
and ask its name together.

Aspire

Crysta Gardner

The world is tired
Its exhaustion forced upon me
Day after day
Gray
Dense, impenetrable, undesired
Spiraling and heavy

A glimpse of light
Snowflakes bursting individuality
Something awakens
Quickens
Planted, swelling, it ignites
Humanity and mentality

Profound visions uniting
one heart, another, then several
A new energy
Memory
Coexisting, balancing, respecting
Love is instrumental.

In the Morning Everything's a Poem

Cindy A. Jones

The cat slides out the door and collapses in a
pool of
striped sun pouring through fence slats,
eyes closed, head to the sky in her prayer.
Plums still green with eastern bellies half flesh
hang in wait of their own descent.
The thunderous opus of crickets long
dispersed, save for one performer who sings soft
now to the sun rather than the moon.
A tiny bird the color of happiness lights in the
tallest tree above my quiet watch;
flits across branches fleeting, considering
no one else is here to witness and yet she exists
still,
like the piano notes coming from next door
muted like a distant memory that
only I can hear.

He Sleeps In The Crook Of My Arm Like A Gosling

Britta Stumpp

He sleeps in the crook of my arm like a gosling
tucked inside a milk-white wing,
like the snow falling outside on trees and
branches
and the moon full above a cloud-smudged sky
in a peace so deep underneath translucent
eyelids,
abalone nails clutching my breast
in the night that is so bright from the
reflection of starlight off the slumbering ground,
a light illuminating the web of tree fingers,
covered in silver, diamond frost.
The tenderness of it all strikes me
a thousand times, a bayonet skewer of
hope and emotion like a switchblade,
through my lungs, only too strong
for real words and the enormity of it all
wrapped tight beside me in this tiny being.
I think of stars and collisions and planets
forming out of dust, congealing to make

and make and make, over and over
and the rightness of it all and its ending
and reforming and lighting across the
dark into ten billion things, enormous
and fragile as a raindrop, frozen in the snow
bank,
clutching to life and to life and to Life,
the rolling tide, ample and boundless,
and infinitely minuscule.
Every night, I experience the Universe in a single
touch.
We are, breathing together, in one breath,
feather lashes touching in the dark,
like the first light in the void, and the snow
outside, the first stars, and I am altered
beyond measure at the beauty of Creation
and the unexplainable Nature of the indomitable
will to Be.

Fire and the Forest

Christina Miller

i.

The trees stood tall as fire struck them
From the outside they appeared to exist no more
But into the earth their life force shot
Stimulating the energy held captive in the roots
The snow came but did not douse the life dance
below
Spring's rainwater kissed the pine seeds and
they began to grow
Saplings spread their roots in the dirt to raise
their limbs up to the sky

Fire does not kill the forest essence
The forest knows how to survive
It adapts and changes even when it seems
That death is all that's left

The forest's nature makes its roots run deep
Its instinct is to survive.
The forest begins to heal and carry on
Regardless what the fire charred from the

forest's soul
The forest knows it is more than what the fire
can burn away

The forest is not afraid of the fire
It is dependent on the fire for survival
The fire clears away the deadwood and
troublesome undergrowth
And cracks the armored shell of the pine trees'
cone
The seeds are free to sow new life
The debris and deadwood was burned to ash
That feeds nourishment to the soil

The spring rain comes to awaken the power of
those roots
The forest is free to grow again
Rising from the ashes to carry life back to the
branches.
Life is what remains

ii.
The thunder brings a new song to the forest
That makes my needles stand on end
The ballads of my ancestors sang of storms

That burn though the forest deep
I'm not sure what comes with this storm
But I have a deep desire to last
The light burns my eyes and shredding metal
rips my ears
A smell I've never known before awakens my
soul
Triggers an instinct from memories of trees past
I must survive

Molten resin rises up from my toes
Through my rings and out my arms
I coat my pinecones with gorgeous glistening
resin
That drips straight from my soul
As the intense heat reaches my feet
Each long toe recoils at the burn
And roots deeper into the ground
The flame laps at my bark
And I hear the crack, sizzle, pop
As my skin turns black from the flame
My glorious evergreen needles singe, squeal,
and curl
As the heat melts them away
Oh yes, there is pain, deep and raw

As the fire tears my existence away
But as it reaches deep into my trunk,

I hear the words of my ancient song
My voice booms strong to join the chorus of fire
The voice reverberates through every bit of
cellulose in my trunk
And the echoes send my pinecones across the
burnt forest floor
The rain comes and the flames die down
But the heat of the embers melts my last bit of
armor
And lick the resin coating away from my pine
seeds
I'm no longer afraid; I've been touched by fire
I've never felt so alive!

The rain is so refreshing
It cleans the ash from my burnt skin
I smell the fresh musty aroma of dirt
I'm so tired, and the dirt is calling me
To tuck myself in to go to sleep
So I close my eyes rooted again in the dirt
Feeling embraced and supported
I still smell the whiffs of smoke

And see the charred carcass of my old self
I am no longer afraid or alone
Tucked in my earthen bed
I feel at home and my snores drift up
To form a new forest song
As I fall deep asleep at peace, knowing
I will survive long after the fire has died.

Hard Alee

Deandra Lanier

There isn't enough time spent discussing
how repeatedly the ropes have to be pulled,
the sheets switched, and the boom tossed
to the other side to reach a destination.

To travel is a jagged lightning bolt
with only a prayer to heave into
the right point on the dock and at a
speed that doesn't obliterate the bow.

I'm floating on rippled happiness,
rocking that empathetic sympathy sadness.
The wind needs to kick up to get anywhere.
On a still day we're left flat, unmoved,
maybe wishing we'd brought a better paddle.
Today, I float on anyway.

Fell

Rin Brighton

there you are.
a tiny whip of a thing
staring me dead in the face with your black
beady eyes
and downturned beak.

you're angry.

of course you are.
pushed out of the nest before all your
downy fluffs were traded for a fuller feather
palette.

you fell.

a fat, plopping raindrop. wanting to fly but
couldn't.
alarmed, you tucked your wings tight, cutting
through air like the whack of an ax;

but you're here.

still.

I can no longer close my eyes without seeing
your dumbstruck face searching mine
as if I were the one who pushed you.

this is not the end. feathers will grow,
you will find your wind,
and soon the sky won't feel so far away.

Fearing Summer's Reveal

Mo Lynn Stoycoff

Everything's going to be okay even
after the blankets are off the bed, even
when my toes are spread, even if
there is only a thin skin of cotton
between me and the world.

Against the cold, the Poorwill lowers
her rocky feathers into the soil and
sleeps. When the heat comes back,
it travels down shaft and vein straight
to her paper pale skin.

It's a shock at first to feel the fingers
of summer slip past her variegated
frock, but then maybe this is when
she remembers all the times she
didn't have to hide.

In Summer

Kelsey Malone

In summer—

Music drifts through open windows
to mingle above the steaming asphalt.
The notes all mix without a DJ:
Mozart's strings with Queen Bey's beats,
Zeppelin's shouts from rusty trucks.

Neighbors can no longer hide,
and offer glimpses of their souls:
the smell of Grandma's berry pie;
bare skin revealing scars and stories;
snippets leaking through screen doors:

". . . thinks Martin might get out of the hospital
soon."

Goose-pimpled children storm the beaches
to splash in lakes as fishermen flee.
No wait at bus stops. No tests. No schedules.
Only sand gritting between their toes,
skin crisped and freckled by sunshine.

Bands play outdoors under painted skies,
thumping songs accompanied
by lousy beer and dripping ice cream.
Our bodies sway together as
sweat slicks our backs and grasping hands.

Cars packed to the brim drive for days
through sun-dappled forests and sunbaked
deserts.
Some trek to family and high school reunions,
to dusty campgrounds and mountaintops.
We thirst for beauty, and we find it.

By fall, the drizzle closes windows,
sending sandals into storage.
No chance encounters and passing smiles.
No deep-fried peanut butter and jellies.
The days, the trees—the world is dying.

Unnatural winter has descended—
flee indoors for months, a year,
so long that neighbors' faces blur,
imperfect in our memories,
some gone for good before the thaw.

But summer—

when flowers, children flood the parks,
and heat and rising gas prices
provide us with collective complaints,
and when we wander through the forests
to sleep under the stars and clouds.

The days stretch longer like a promise:
this too shall pass, all things must end.
We'll stand again in summer soon,
drawn from this daze of deadly winter.
Our souls, humanity awaken—

in summer.

Hope

Alice Ramona Font

Lately, my life has been a cross between a
tornado and an earthquake.
I try to stretch into this new form that is being
created by the pressure.

Ideas bubble up from the center of my being,
and if I am aware and notice, it helps.
It can be a song, a joke,
a rock or crystal or a favorite magazine, and I
remember
for the next time I feel lost or powerless.

My life is not a cross between a tornado and an
earthquake.
It is only my perception of the moment and
circumstances.
I can be at peace anytime I choose,
and I choose peace more often.

There is a word that is light and like gossamer
wings

and yet is the underpinning of all that is strong
and resilient.

That word is hope.
May you find it.
Or, better yet,
May it find you.

New Shoes

Christina Miller

A new dance between foot and shoe. It is time to begin. To take the first step. The leather is stiff and resists as the movement arches from my toes to my heels. There are no creases yet to ease the bend of the toes. The newness brings doubt that these shoes will ever fit. Are they too tight, is my pinky toe going to rub, are the soles too hard? Won't know the answers until I start to walk.

I've kept these shiny new loafers in their winter box. It's time to break in their soles. Crisp brown leather stitched together by robotic arms. Tough stable rubber treads that have yet to touch the ground.

Slip in a foot; feel each seam rub along my skin. Stretch out the toes to find the space to move. Thread the laces through each eyelet, and tie a sturdy square knot. Slowly lower each foot to the ground. Feel the bones spread in my feet as gravity pulls me fully into the shoe.

The shoes I wore all winter molded to my feet. I slipped the shoes on each morning to tread whatever winter threw at me. The soles fought the cold, and ice and grew thin from the fight. A dark stain spread across the toes from walking through salt and melted snow. The leather formed deep ravines at my big toe to allow for full movement of my feet.

They kept me safe through the worst of winter's storm. My feet knew each seam and stitch like an old friend. But as seasons change, the life of these trusty shoes comes to an end. Their dance is over.

Unsoiled, stiff, raw, I take the first step. It's not comfortable, my feet long for my old shoes. They push against the hard leather screaming, "Give me space! Let me move." The shoes resist back, wanting to cling to the shape of the mold that forged them. I know I need to take the first steps and keep moving. This is not my first dance. This dance started with my baby shoes.

Nothing is easy with those first steps, and my

feet are going to ache. Hell, the stiff leather is probably going to rip the skin from my ankle since the leather pattern doesn't match where my old callus formed. But I'm accustomed to new shoes. I know what to expect. I know I can do it. I've done this dance many times before.

The leather starts to stretch. My feet start to learn the dance of these new shoes. The shoes grow pliable and adapt as they hug to my feet.

That perfect dance between my feet and the shoes, where the shoe has formed to my feet and my toes know each seam, where the leather is still shiny and the sole is firm and stable, only lasts for a moment.

New shoes become old shoes. My feet experience a new pain, the pain from the shoes worn thin. No longer able to support the weight of the dance.

Too stiff, too hard, too new will soon pass to worn out, tread bare, and seams broken through. Each dance is different from the one before. The

memory of the last dance clings to my feet as
they break in a new pair, but I know I will make
it through.

Behind Closed Doors

Jonathan Tysor

Have you ever kept a secret from your peers
To feel the guilt and pain?
Try keeping one for years,
Being driven absolutely insane.

Darkness. Trapped in a room. It's all I know.
I see the light, but I'm fearful to go.
The silver doorknob taunts me
with its enticing iridescent glow

This alluring passage needs no key.
It is the key.
This door is the key to finally set me free.

Free from this pain,
Free from the spinning driving me insane,
Free from the countless nights with no sleep,
Free from the thoughts that cause me to weep,
Free from this guilt.
"I'm ready," I say.
I reach for the door but, like a flower, I wilt.

The sun shines through, and the mask comes on
awhile.
People stare at my bright sunflower smile.
Sure, I'm happy. Why not?
Maybe because I'm left here to rot.

Maybe because they're out there and I'm not.
Maybe because they all forgot.
Forgot about us.

Forgot about how it's not alright. "It's 2019."
Yippee for 2019!
Where people have the audacity to be mean
yet don't have the guts to do it
without the protection of their screen.
Their unseen faces ruining lives
Driving people to the edge of hysteria
And that's only America.

If not for the wretched glass barrier,
I could be freer, happier, merrier.
I reach for the knob once more
though the outside is riskier, scarier.

My hand trembles tremendously,

My palms flood with rivers of sweat.
I turn the knob, ready to go . . . Regret.
Slam! The door shuts tight.
And a bright future is out of sight.

Every night, I dream of that future
in my cold, dark room.
Dreaming to escape the misery and gloom.
To grow, to blossom, to be a bright flower and
bloom!
And to inform society of the chaotic doom.

Illegal in 72 countries.
Offer to support, help with "therapies."
I don't need therapy for being me.
There shouldn't be punishment.
Why the death penalty?

Death penalty in eight countries.
Country definition: people of a nation.
Nation definition: large body of people united.
I don't believe it's an obligation for the people
of a nation to kill one another.

Back again, hand shaking more than before.

I've committed, I'm done fighting this war.
Creak. The door knob turns once more.
Step. I've got one foot out the door.

I can smell the sweet air and hear the sweet sound.
The feeling of victory, touching the ground.
This is the point where I turn around.
Not today.

I don't want to.
I can't hide anymore.
It's time to step out of the closet door.

Happy Hour

Mo Lynn Stoycoff

This is when I retreat to the jewel blue sofa with
its red pillows
where the Yorkie/Schnauzer mix sits with
commanding impatience,
knowing that he is fully entitled to this hour in
my day.

I close the white linen curtains, a thrift store
find.
My nine plants strain toward the window like a
crowd
not wanting to leave a particularly excellent
show.
The light has changed from manic afternoon sun
to buttery comfort.
The guitar in its stand makes a shadow that
looks like people.

I stretch my legs over the edge, and he puts his
nose on my knee.

My eyes are taking a break from screens. My ears find the quiet.
I could keep going. I can always keep going. My nature is to seek trouble.

There were many years of restless mistakes before I made this nest.
Many homes, some shared. Many things broken and thrown away.
This is the first piece of furniture I ever bought new,
one that has only known the weight of me—plus this little brown dog,
who in this ordinary moment is doing the daily work of saving my life.

My Boys

Beverly Bradley

My boys have always been a source of aggravation and affection. But on one terrible night, they also gave me hope.

My younger son, Shawn, has battled Crohn's disease since he was a teen. There was a time when it looked as if the disease had finally gotten the upper hand.

Fetched to Utah from California by his brother Chris, Shawn was rushed into emergency surgery. During the surgery, his colon disintegrated and had to be removed. Even worse, as the colon was being removed it totally fell apart, dumping the contents into his digestive cavity.

Shawn did well with the surgery, but the complications resulted in a prolonged hospitalization and a transfer to the University of Utah's infectious disease unit. Eventually, he was moved to a long-term care facility in Bountiful.

Shawn's weight plummeted, dropping to less than 100 pounds.

Despair was my new best friend. Shawn didn't like eating or drinking, so he didn't. Worst of all, the rebellious light he'd always had in his eyes not only dimmed but disappeared.

The loss of my son seemed something I had to prepare for. There is no way to prepare to lose a child. The world tilted and fell away. Suddenly, the earth was flat and I was balanced on the edge, trying to hang on with just my toes as an endless abyss hovered beneath me. I didn't want to give up, but didn't know what to do.

And then there was Chris. He was not going to give up, and he began a quiet plan to save his brother. He told me he had entered Shawn in a contest sponsored by a local radio station—three contestants a day played an original song, and the winner was awarded a new guitar.

Shawn had been a musician for years, but now he had no guitar and no reason, in his mind, to live.

The contest seemed like the perfect idea, but there were many obstacles for Shawn, mainly transportation and permission to leave the facility. Chris went about quietly removing every obstacle, and on the day of the contest, he picked his brother up and took him to the radio station. Shawn won the competition and returned to the care facility with his new guitar.

He came back to a hero's welcome. The long-term facility is largely populated with elderly patients, and they cheered and clapped upon his return. He made a tour of the hospital, giving a mini-concert on each floor.

When I visited that night, the change was readily visible. His eyes alight, he played his song again for his family and passersby. His progress was steady after that, and Chris was there, teasing and encouraging him every step of the way.

I remember looking into his eyes and seeing the light had come back on. I walked outside and looked at stars and thanked my higher power.

Chris had saved his brother. He had found a way to reach him. And when Chris came up behind me, put his arms around me, and said, "It's going to be okay," for the first time in weeks I thought it just might.

The Home Within

Kathleen Bradford

Do you remember watching the night sky? Did it call to you, beckoning you home? But you knew you couldn't leave, couldn't even visit. You had work to do, important work. Your soul was needed here for many to be touched by the power you channel, their hearts and minds put at peace when you put a piece of your light into them, and the dance begins. Shimmering brightly, traveling this world through all the beings you have ever met, all those that show up to assist you on your journey and all those yet to come. The light you share is eternal, has existed from the beginning of time. It is now but awakened.

Deep Breaths

Lindsey Bakke

Deep breath in. Hold. Deep Breath out. Hold.
Repeat until the shaking in my hands begins to
stop. The pounding of my heart begins to slow.
The pressure in my chest begins to ease.

Deep breath in. Hold. Deep breath out. Hold. It's
going to be okay. Today's a new day. My
demons won't win.

Deep breath in. Hold. Deep breath out. How I
wish my demons were real. Flesh and blood.
Then I could fight them. End them. End this. But
my demons are of my own making. My mind
has no problem highlighting the damage done.
The cracks made wide. The pieces missing. Pain
and fear. Guilt. Anxiety. Hatred, and at the very
far side of it all, love.

Deep breath in. Hold. Deep breath out. Hold.
The sun is here. The world isn't so bleak. The
light hides the shadows, and yet some part of me

yearns for the shade. It's easier to hide in the dark. The weight of the world doesn't sit so heavy on my shoulders. The earth quiets. Reminds me I'm alright. For some of the biggest evils never come in the night.

Deep breath in. Hold. Deep breath out. There. The turmoil is calming. The raging seas of emotions still. Level out. Release me.

Deep breath in. Hold. Deep breath out. Life was never meant to be easy. Never meant to be full of joy. This pain is okay. This fear is okay. It means I'm here. It means I'm alive. It means I have one more day to thrive.

Deep breath in. Hold. Deep breath out. The corners of my lips ease into a smile. My eyes finally open.

Deep breath in. It's time to go.

Knowing

Cindy A. Jones

You find yourself
awake in the dark of night
wondering if you're choosing the right things,
if your life is paying the right kind of tribute
to your soul.
Knowing
there is Knowing to be had.

Like when you realize
your craving for rain, the kind that soothes
tempers
in the deep August heat,
is no different than your wish for sun,
the kind that burns through
to your bones
in the gray of January.

Laying out easy answers
like cool, white cloths on fevers;
change of weather, change of pace, change of
circumstance

are only stories you tell yourself.
Temporary liberation.
It's not the rain or the sun
you crave.
It's the variation.

Why We Long for Forgotten Things

Deandra Lanier

Nostalgia is that dust you see in the light
as it's passing through old dirty glass;
that window looking out to the crashing surf,
banks beating back against rocky pastures
and the sound of anticipation counted by waves.

When anything begins, whether it's the
water's rise and crest or a conversation,
it must fall and wash and reiterate.
The beauty of it is that the ocean is always
moving, and the wind blows somewhere.

Let us envision a world where the wind is
blowing
through an unending aspen grove.
Let us not forget that we are all sharing the same
roots.

A world must be possible where, as your leaves
fall

atop mine on the cool earth and an American
Robin
passes from my perch to yours,
we reach toward one another still.

The Only Thing

Kathleen Bradford

The only thing I am responsible for understanding are my own emotions, my own motives, and my own belief systems as they pertain to me becoming the best version of myself. The rest is simply having compassion and acceptance of what I don't understand, and loving it anyway.

Unbroken

Vince Font

Nothing's ever broken beyond repair
As long as there's a willingness to fix it when it
breaks.
And just because something breaks doesn't
mean it's garbage.
I think of all the things I own,
Broken in some way:
The watch that told the time once long ago when
my grandfather held my hand;
A poster from my youth that's held together on
the wall with scotch tape and memories.
And finally, me,
Broken in ways I'll never understand.
Cracked in places I'll never have time to fix.
I won't throw me away
As long as there's a chance that I still work.

Conceiving Hope

R.S. Veira

My goal every morning before climbing out of bed is to give birth to hope, and most days it's a joyous experience. But some days, it's a laborious task. Just existing is a burden on these peculiar mornings. The day's obstacles are daunting, and the pains from yesterday are still fresh.

It's on these mornings that my mind replays my life's lowlights: a compilation of times when I said the wrong thing, hurt someone I loved, or fumbled an opportunity. These thoughts escort me into the darkness. A darkness that's strangely comfortable and provides perverse pleasure while wallowing in it. Soon, I'm seriously considering canceling all plans, going back to bed, and giving up on the day. I begin to convince myself that life is meaningless, people are detestable, and the world is beyond saving. I plunge further into the darkness and consider if life is even worth living.

Yet when all seems lost, there's a glimmer in the darkness. This glimmer could be anything;

most times it's an uplifting memory of God's faithfulness. Whatever it may be, it offers a way out of the darkness. For the briefest of moments, hope shines and is conceived. I then find myself at a crossroads. I can either go the distance and carry hope to term or continue into the abyss.

My friends, when we are faced with such a dilemma, we must gird our loins and embrace the light. We must muster the courage and leave the darkness. We must give birth to hope. I've learned that if allowed, hope grows rapidly after conception. That glimmer becomes a refulgent beam of light that guides us out of the abyss.

As hope gestates, I'm reminded of moments when life was sweet and made my heart hum. I remember the joy of achieving a dream, falling in love, or laughing in the company of good friends. Hope facilitates new perspectives, and I see the once daunting tasks of the day as ingeniously designed opportunities. I reconsider my contempt for my fellow man and realize we're all just doing our best. As hope nears delivery, it's clear that the world is worth saving, and we each have a part to play in its salvation.

For when hope is born, it paves the way for

faith, and faith provides the strength to love. Imbued with this strength, we can shine light into the darkness of the world and help lead others out of the abyss. Through the strength of our love, we exemplify to others the transformative power of hope and the necessity of its birth.

So, my friends, on those days when you find yourself lost in the darkness but see that glimmer of hope, take hold.

Allow it to grow.

Earth Rising

Susan L. Prescott

Our first glimpse of the luminous and fragile beauty of planet Earth—as a blue jewel in the vastness of space—was a transcendent moment in human history. The "Earthrise" photograph, taken by astronaut Bill Anders on the 1968 Apollo 8 mission, became one of the most significant images of the 20th Century. It gave a new and very significant perspective. And new hope. "We came all the way to the Moon to discover Earth," he reflected on the moment that shifted collective

human consciousness. We saw our home. One planet.
For all people. Glowing with the delicate layer of life
enfolding her. Dynamic and wondrous in her beauty.
A miracle. Transformative in triggering a profound
shift in both environmental awareness and the
potential for human unity. Whenever we see our home
from this perspective it seems utterly illogical that we
are gouging the Earth for resources that are spent so
wastefully and in large part on conflict, weaponry, and
destruction. We should all take a look at that
photograph from time to time.

*   *   *

Across the desolate cratered dust of the Moon's
surface, we see the darkness of the void. But the
darkness is filled with love and awe. And there
we see a blue ball of light, of oceans and swirling
clouds. Rising. Half unseen but coming into light.
Distant but so intimate in the feelings it stirs, as
though looking back at ourselves across countless
lifetimes. Looking into our own hearts to see the
future. From here, we can see that everything is
interconnected. Not just in this moment, but
across all of time. And as we all look at this

distant view of ourselves together, we hold the same vantage, in unity. This is where we should come from time to time. For here, there is great peace. Great wisdom.

From here we can imagine. We can rise through the entrenched stories that have limited our sense of possibility. We can let go of fear, doubt, and cynicism and allow ourselves to dream. Allow ourselves to be free. Nothing can stop the power of our love and imagination. We hold out our arms as though to embrace the magnificent beauty before us. We feel love for its wholeness and know it is part of us, just as we are part of all things. From here it is so easy to love. To feel connected to everything and everyone. Oneness. Even as we turn our eyes to the Universe beyond, we no longer feel dwarfed by its vastness. Because we are made from "the stuff of the stars." We are not small or insignificant, because we are part of this vast greatness.

From here we can question what we believe to be true. We can let go of the limiting assumptions we have made about ourselves and about each other. About reality and what is possible. Things may not really be as we have always assumed. Or the truth of them may be so much greater than we have understood. As we allow our horizons to expand, so too does the truth. So too does our reality.

Our heart, like the Earthrise, is still not all fully into view, but the part still unseen is infinitely greater and coming into light. We have gone to the Moon to discover the Earth, just as we can now go out into the world, the Universe, to discover what lies within.

*   *   *

Sometimes, when I speak of the need to see this "bigger picture," people express the counterpoint that we should not lose touch with "reality." But there is little risk of that. With most of our energy and attention focused on the challenges of planetary change, and the challenges of everyday life, we are naturally "grounded." In fact, I believe that taking a deeper view is not losing touch—rather, it is gaining greater perspective. We are endlessly bombarded with the negativity, obstacles, and cynicism of "realism." My purpose, in work and in all my life, has been to balance this with hope, enthusiasm, and entirely realistic possibility. This is not to deny the difficulties or be unrealistic about the challenges that we face, but to take a more balanced perspective that encompasses the opportunity and possibility that they simultaneously bring. There is nothing wrong with having our minds in the stars as our feet are on the ground. We can span the distance—and achieve far more that way.

To overcome our greatest challenges, we must address the value systems that created them in the first place. And fundamentally question the way we choose to live on our planet. How we see ourselves. How we see each other. How we care for our place and our communities. And how we approach our challenges.

In an era of so many "broken systems," we must equally address the "broken spirit." Too often our focus is on "the worst" of human nature in creating adversity on all scales, only perpetuating despair and hopelessness. We have devalued the power of "the best" of human nature—the very things that unite, empower, and refocus priorities of individuals and societies—

failing to see this as fundamental to all our challenges and our greatest asset in overcoming them.

It is time.

Time to inspire hope, purpose, and optimism by imagining a better future.

Time to revalue the power of kindness, empathy, love, and mutual respect—and their importance in health and resilience on all scales

Time to question what we value as progress and how we define growth.

Time to rediscover our love of nature—and the awe, wonder, joy, compassion this inspires

Time to restore our communities and build grassroots efforts toward meaningful change, and time to understand our connectivity and the interdependence of our problems and the solutions.

Time to realize our hope.

But to truly evolve, we much also challenge the "hope" of those who seek to capitalize on chaos for greed and person gain or manipulate others to maintain the unhealthy status quo. That requires placing far greater value on deeper wisdom and meaningful purpose—which have also been neglected and eroded. The aftermath of the "mass trauma" associated with the many events of 2020, may allow new opportunities for large-scale post-traumatic growth, a re-appraisal of values, higher levels of environmental and social concern, awareness of new possibilities, and greater shared wisdom.

Challenges, like the pandemic, that break the status quo can provide new or accelerated opportunities for change. Acute events can unmask chronic problems that seemed impossible to overcome or may not have even been recognized. The new perspectives and greater awareness that result can create new possibilities and galvanize action. Traumatic events can act as catalysts that accelerate growth and change through new awareness and new opportunities that might not have occurred—or taken much longer. What seemed impossible becomes essential.

This applies to personal growth but may apply equally at collective scales. Our personal growth and empowerment also go hand in hand with collective community benefits. These are equally important and synergistic—but all change ultimately starts with individuals. Social change does not have to be framed around "personal sacrifice" but can instead be viewed in terms of how making these commitments, taking responsibility, and changing our attitudes are in fact empowering and rewarding for individuals. This can answer our deeper yearning for something better and something greater. This is where the power is. Attitudes are the things that we *can* change—and quickly—*if* we choose.

There is something very powerful in our sense of community and feeling that "everyone and everything is in this together"—something that is progressively under threat with growing divisiveness and social isolation. We seem to be forgetting that the very process of working together to solve these problems will bring its own rewards and satisfaction. From that vantage point, our greatest challenges are also creating our greatest opportunities to change how we do things and work together on a global scale in ways we never have before. There can be a strange beauty in adversity that is deepened by a shared quest—even though we created the problems in the first place.

This need for cohesion may now be driven by necessity—but it is nonetheless a critical opportunity to step forward together. In other words, *the very journey* to these solutions will bring the community cohesion and unity of purpose that we are currently lacking. This is the very time that we need great boldness and bravery of vision to overcome our personal fears and the fear and polarization that permeates our world. The undercurrents of every challenge, every triumph, are played out on every level. What applies in our personal transformation, applies to our community, applies to our planet. The same patterns. Like fractals. What we learn about ourselves we can apply to *everything* else. It gives connection, relevance, and meaning to everything. We are already using our interconnectivity for many large-scale benefits, and this will only increase. Our perspectives, our awareness, our willingness to learn and grow, have the power to accelerate this.

Imagining the future is the first step to getting there. It is not hard to see what needs to be changed. But nothing will happen unless we decide to change it—and allow ourselves to imagine what it could look like. For this, we can take inspiration from the power of "Earthrise" as one of the most transcendent moments in modern history—when we first saw the Earth across the void of space. We can be reminded of the profound wonder and awe, it ignited. How it inspired a renewed desire for peace, unity, justice, and appreciation and care for nature. How it revealed that we are more aligned in our vision and desire for a better world than our current polarized social climate suggests—especially when we are inspired.

We are on the cusp of something great. But we must reach out and choose it. In doing so, we will cross another transcendent threshold to a new era of possibility—and new hope. We might all begin by asking ourselves "What kind of world do we want to live in?"

It is time.

The Old Stump

Vince Font

These are the remains of an old stump in my backyard. Once it was a tree, but now it's not. At first I didn't like it. But now I do. It has its own unique beauty. And a sort of rugged stubbornness that says, "Hey! I'm still here." It makes me see how the things we are leave lasting marks, and not always in a bad way. I want to be just like the stump when I'm no longer a tree.

A Word About the Students of Pleasant Hope Academy

During our open call for submissions, we were fortunate to have been contacted by Nightingale Wakigera, a registered nurse and child advocate working on the behalf of the students of Pleasant Hope Academy in Kikuyu, Kenya. The written submissions we received from these children were everything you might expect from young writers. They were imperfect and they were raw, but they contained one of the most critically important elements all writers should endeavor to bring to the page. They contained pure, unspoiled truth. And every word thrummed with the vibrant, beating heart of life. It is our privilege to be able to present to you the writings of the students of the Grade 4 class of Pleasant Hope Academy.

Our School

Nelly Kendi

Our school is Pleasant Hope Academy. It is found in Kamangu sub-location, Karai location, Kikuyu District, Kiambu County in Kenya.

We have several buildings in our school, which include the girls' dormitory, the boys' dormitory, the dining hall, various class rooms, the office, the one-story building that holds the library, and the rest of the classrooms.

Our school compound is very clean and beautiful, with the well-kept flowerbeds and also the beautiful paintings on the walls. Some of the flowers are roses, daisies, Amaranthus, Amaryllis, Angel Eyes, and Argyranthemum.

We have a lot of trees that surround our school. This helps to give a very cool breeze. We have a school garden where vegetables are grown, some of which include broccoli, cauliflower, Chinese cabbage, and other sweet vegetables.

We also have a greenhouse where tomatoes and onions are grown. We do not purchase vegetables but enjoy them fresh from the garden.

Cleanliness is very important; we always ensure that our school compound is well cleaned. We maintain high levels of cleanliness in the dormitories and our classrooms, which are well-organized. This is to help us have a good stay in school and a conducive environment for learning.

When it comes to our teachers, they are very friendly and encouraging. They teach us very well, such that all the pupils understand what they are taught. We always maintain a high level of respect to our teachers.

Some of the subjects taught in our school are mathematics, English, Kiswahili, science, social studies, and CRE. We also have chess and music lessons.

When it comes to the national examination, our school emerges among the top schools in the sub-county. In 2018, we were the best school in our sub-county. We look forward to better performance in this year's examinations, since we have been promised a trip to the coast.

We have different clubs in our school, which include the scouting club, music club, Ngonjera club (a Swahili poem), chess club, Bible club, young farmers, knitting club, talent club, sewing club, poetic club, and dance club.

In 2020, when we had to stay at home due COVID-19, I had a difficult time at home because the environment was not conducive for learning. I missed being in school, where I knew that I would get three meals every day.

I missed my friends from school, the ones we talk about dreams of the future with, the ones we play with, sing and dance with, and help each other with school work.

I missed the teachers who teach and discipline us with so much love. I pray that the vaccine will work and we can go back to the life we had before the virus.

When we came back from the long break, we found so many changes in our school, and it was a great surprise. Our dormitories look so wonderful—they are more spacious, and our bathrooms are more beautiful. It is so much easier to keep them clean. Even though our classrooms are now fewer because we have to keep social distance during learning, we got tents that serve as classrooms for now, and we pray for more permanent classrooms since harsh weather will be a challenge during learning.

We love our school very much, and we also love our friends who are in America; we always pray for them.

Our school is the best and will always be in our minds. BRAVO PLEASANT HOPE ACADEMY!

Unity, Hope, and Positivity

Victor Onyango

Attention! Attention! Attention!
Please give me your ears,
This thing is seriously contagious,
Spreading for less than a minute,
Surely Coronavirus is not a joke.

A highly infectious, killer disease,
A specialized human-life hunter,
Killing over thousands of lives in a minute,
Brothers and sisters, this thing is serious,
Surely Coronavirus is not a joke.

Sneezing and coughing,
Difficulties during breathing,
High body temperatures and flu-like symptoms,
Some of the signs and symptoms of COVID-19,
Surely Coronavirus is not a joke.

A slogan states embrace women avoid men,
For safety and avoidance of contraction,
Avoid touching your eyes, nose and mouth,

Wash your hands regularly with soap and
running water,
Surely Coronavirus is not a joke.

Secondly always keep social distance,
Oh! Without forgetting to wear your mask!
For these are the assurances of safety,
Dear loved ones, don't take it for granted,
Surely Coronavirus is not a joke.

But how can we overcome it?
The brave stated: unity is strength,
Together as citizens this thing is communal,
It is mine and yours and everyone's else's,
Surely Coronavirus is not a joke.

Corona kills regardless of age, religion and
gender,
But if we work together, it will be defeated,
Unity is the ease of all problems,
Let's help out the vulnerable,
Surely Coronavirus is not a joke.

It's a killer world pandemic,
But there is a glimmer of hope,

The World Health Organization is on toes,
Working hard to get a vaccine,
Surely Coronavirus is not a joke.

Positivity during this time will really help,
This thing has brought up a new culture,
Wearing of masks was done in industries only,
Now everyone must wear it always,
Surely Coronavirus is not a joke.

A worldwide disease has brought effects,
Some are negative others are positive,
It has led to closing of institutions,
Learning, religion, and travel has stopped,
Surely Coronavirus is not a joke.

This pandemic should not be taken for granted,
It made people worldwide suffer,
Some losing their jobs others giving up in life,
Surely this brought desperation to the people,
Surely Coronavirus is not a joke.

On the other side it has put,
Families, members of the community intact,
children now enjoy parental care,

Indoor activities also get a chance to be played,
Surely Coronavirus is not a joke.

Parents, teachers and guardians,
Students, pupils and school leavers,
Whoever you are, responsibilities is in our
hands,
To flatten the curve, we need to have unity, hope
and positivity,
Surely Coronavirus is not a joke.

Story of Hope, Unity and Positivity

Muiruri Mukuria and Linah Gaichugi

This is a true story that will make most of you shed tears. It is the story of a girl called Vumilivu. She was born in 2008 under two parents who ever quarreled. Her mother was a no-nonsense woman who never cared about her children's lives.

One chilly evening, the parents reached home as usual. They had not been on good terms, since the woman had been having an extramarital affair. That night, the parents started quarreling and fought in front of the children.

They ended up parting, and the children, who were both girls, were left in the hands of their father. At that moment, the father had been beaten up to the point of nose bleeding. The elder daughter, called Tumaini, was old enough and prepared supper for her sister and her father. They ate the supper and rested in their beds.

That night, hell broke loose, and everything turned up for Vumilivu's father. A group of men reached the home and asked for the father.

Tumaini bravely tried to prevent them from getting into the house, but her efforts bore no fruits. The men beat up the children's father and dragged him out in the cold as he groaned in pain.

The following morning, Vumilivu's mother came and tried to kill the two girls. Tumaini tried her best to hide Vumilivu because she was only a toddler.

As Vumilivu was trying to crawl away, her mother got hold of the tin paraffin lamp, which was their only source of light, and threw it at her, landing it on her back.

Paraffin on her clothes caught fire and burned Vumilivu. On seeing this, their mother left. Tumaini was left alone, tears rolling down her cheeks as she watched her sister cry in pain. She did not hesitate but took a wet cloth and wiped her.

The burial of their father was one of sadness, and no one was willing to take the girls. They were to be left alone in a cold, muddy house.

Back then, Vumilivu and Tumaini thought their lives had come to an end. Little did they know they were created for a purpose.

By grace, their aunt Mary took them in. She also took Vumilivu to the hospital. Mary, whom the children now identified as their mother, did her best to bring up the sisters together with her own children.

For our Creator knows everything about us, there was a kind-hearted woman called Margaret Njoki. Margaret was led by the love of children to help Aunt Mary, and the two women agreed to work hand in hand to help the girls.

After some time, the sisters were sponsored and taken to a school in Kiambu county called Pleasant Hope Academy. This took place in 2017, and the girls began a new life.

They have worked hard, and today Tumaini is in Class Six, whereas Vumilivu is in Class Five. They have a good flow of life. They are living in peace.

This opportunity has helped Vumilivu identify her talent in music. She has even tried to compose her own songs. She is good at playing the piano and also the flute.

Tumaini, on the other hand, is good in football and in class. She is a quick grasper of things. For the unity that Margaret and Mary have, the two girls do not lack peace and joy in them.

The sisters have agreed to live without ever thinking about their parents but only of their future lives. 'Til today, Vumilivu looks at the scars on her back and sheds tears.

The sisters comfort each other and try not to remember the past. They are grateful to the Almighty for saving them from their mother, and they have hope of going on with their lives with the help of the two kind ladies who love them as their own.

Tumaini and Vumilivu are positive that their future is bright, and that they will one day be able to help other people.

Story of Hope, Unity and Positivity

Mumbi Mokeira Mukuria

There is always hope, even when things seem to be falling apart. Wonders will never end in this world we live in; indeed, everything was created for a purpose, and it's for that very purpose that we exist.

This happened in our beautiful country, Kenya, some years ago. A creature that one could not have imagined did something that surprised many. It was a normal stray dog seen carrying a green polythene bag and moving from one place to another.

Seeing this, some villagers got curious and wondered what could have been in the bag, so they snatched it from the dog.

On opening it, they were shocked to see what was inside: a beautiful baby girl. Luckily, she was still alive.

They rushed the baby to Kenyatta National Hospital, where she was received by nurses in wonder but with open arms. She was treated, and in a few days she was okay. The nurses called her Angel.

Imagine going from being thrown away to die in a pit to being a healthy, bouncing baby girl.

The event got the attention of a couple, who came and adopted the girl. Today, the couple lives with the miraculous girl who was saved by the grace of the Creator, who created the dog and the baby.

Who Will Understand the Children?

Who who! Will ever understand the children!
When I eat too much, they say I am fat.
When I eat too little, they say I am thin.
Then who, who will ever understand the
children?

When I talk too much, they say I am a parrot.
When I talk less, they say I am dumb.
Then who, who will ever understand the
children?

But in school, I am embraced by the teachers
With open arms and love.
They have all the time
To listen to my worries,
happiness or sadness.
I have hope.
Teachers have time to understand the children.

Written by the Grade 4 Class of Pleasant Hope Academy: Alex Njenga, Brighton Githua, Charles Njuguna, Collins Waithaka, Faith Njoki, Faith Njambi, Joseph Kibiro, Jeffy Kagwe, Joy Wanjiku, Lucy Wambui, Mary Wambui, Precious Wambui, Stanley Thairu, Tanisha Karega, Peter Kariuki.

About the Authors

C.W. Allen is a Midwestern transplant to Utah's West Desert, where she serves as a chapter president of the League of Utah Writers. She writes fantasy novels for tweens, picture books for children, and short stories and poems for former children. She is also a frequent guest presenter at writing conferences and club meetings, which helps her procrastinate knuckling down to any actual writing. Keep up with her latest projects at cwallenbooks.com.

Lindsey Bakke enjoys writing when adulting becomes exhausting and she needs a break from reality, that is unless her hands are full with horses or dogs. She's spent her life working with animals and explored much of the world with the U.S. Navy. She been inspired by the stories she's found in her many travels, as well as from the personal experiences that can only be gained when you're far from the safety of home. (LindseyBakke.com)

Kathleen Bradford is a writer of multi-dimensional beauty and has been composing and writing stories since she was in grade school. Writing pen to paper, not knowing what will happen on the next page, she takes great pleasure in watching her stories unfold before her. She is the published author of the ongoing Gateways series; first set being: The Light Worker, The Shadow Chasers and Song of Dragons. She is also an enthusiastic star gazer and thoroughly enjoys exploring every faucet of the beauty and complexity in nature on this planet and in all worlds beyond us.

Beverly Bradley has been writing since she could read. She worked for eighteen years in small-town newspapers across Southern California, focused mostly on government, crime, and features. She returned to Utah some twenty-two years ago after missing the mountains and the seasons. Beverly retired three years ago and has various writing projects underway.

Rin Brighton is an author living in Utah with her husband and small children. Although she studied to become a special educator at university, the past few troublesome years have reignited her passions of writing and art. Rin has always had a fascination with words. Stories and poetry have helped her find a light in the difficulty and struggles of daily life. Thanks to her wonderfully supportive husband and family, she has published two poetry collections (*The Stars Have Eyes* and *Penumbra*), a young adult novel (*The Dismantlement of Fallon Midler*), and two more works which will be available in 2022.

Dr. Yuria Celidwen is of Indigenous Nahua and Maya descent from the highlands of Chiapas, Mexico. She works on the intersection of Indigenous studies, cultural psychology, and contemplative science, investigating the embodied experience of self-transcendence and how it enhances prosocial behavior in world Indigenous contemplative traditions. Her "Ethics of Belonging" thesis offers an earth-based ecology that engenders wellness and purpose through relational ecological awareness. She emphasizes the reclamation, revitalization, and transmission of Indigenous wisdom and the advancement of Indigenous and planetary rights. (yuriacelidwen.com)

Alice Ramona Font is a mother of four, a grand-mother of five, a great-grandmother of one, and a relocated Southern belle who has lived in Northern California since 1980. She is proud to have given birth to two successful writers.

Crysta Gardner lives in North Ogden, Utah. Although she doesn't consider herself much of a poet, she was drawn to participate in this anthology in the hope of shining a bit of light amid so much darkness. She loves her kids, her husband, her family, friends, and pets unwaveringly. Anytime she can break away from everyday toils, you'll find her out in nature—hiking, camping, adventuring, or just sitting among the trees.

Cindy A. Jones is a freelance writer, marketer, graphic designer, and self-proclaimed "seeker of ordinary miracles." She writes poetry and fiction in order to connect with the natural world and to keep any modicum of sanity while raising two teenage daughters.

Deandra Lanier, U of U graduate, resides in Utah with her husband and two kids. These poems come from feeling a lot of love for the beauty in things, even when it's hard. She works in retail, where she finds small joys in things like the silly details of a stranger's discarded shopping list. She finds life's largest joys in her two children and getting to know good people. The rest is, mostly, poetry.

Kelsey Malone is a copywriter by day and a wannabe novelist by night. She studied Creative Writing at Utah State University and now lives in Seattle, where she enjoys hiking, lattes, and other typical pursuits found in the beautiful Pacific Northwest.

Christina Miller is a writer and photographer. She has written for *Indie Ogden* and the Ogden *Standard Examiner*. She helped curate the *PoetFlow Anthology* published by Glass Spider Publishing, and is published in the anthology as well.

Christina is also an active supporter of the arts in Ogden.

Susan L. Prescott is an artist, writer, pediatrician and professor of medicine. Globally, she is recognized for her interdisciplinary work for ecological and social justice, promoting mutualistic value systems for healthier people, places and planet. She integrates art into both her scientific work and her advocacy—to underscore the importance of creativity, imagination, and inspiration in fashioning new narratives for hope, self-awareness and wellness on all scales. She is also the founding president of inVIVO Planetary Health. (drsusanprescott.com)

Mo Lynn Stoycoff is an autodidactic writer and poet whose work has appeared or is forthcoming in *Poetry Now, Rise Up Review, South Broadway Ghost Society, California Quarterly, Speckled Trout Review* and many other journals and anthologies. Mo works in the performing arts and lives in Central California. (molynstoycoff.com)

Brittanië "Britta" Visser Stumpp is a mother, wife, yogi, graphic designer, teacher, and poet. She has a Bachelor's in Secondary English/Creative Writing from Weber State University, a Broadcast Journalism and Electronic Media degree from Weber State University, and a Graphic and Web Design Associate's from Eagle Gate College. She also holds a Yoga Philosophy certificate from Oregon State University. She began writing poetry at a young age to make sense of the world. She has been published in several journals and magazines. Her book of poetry, *Kindred Matter*, was published in 2019. Britta lives in Ogden, Utah, with her son and her husband, Adrian Stumpp, who is also a writer.

Jonathan Tysor is an actor, aspiring screenwriter, midnight baker, overthinker, and avid yogi. Having finished high school early, he is now attending Dodge College of Film and Media Arts at Chapman University as a screenwriting major. Passionate about social justice and making a difference, he believes in using films as a platform to highlight underrepresented topics.

This poem was written as a creative way of coming out to his family and peers at age 15.

R.S. Veira, born Raphael Sylvester Veira, is an author, director, and self-proclaimed dreamer. He is the co-founder of Dream With Me Productions, a production company in Los Angeles, California. He is also the founder of RSV Ink, a publishing imprint of Dream With Me Productions. Veira is the author of five books and has written and directed two short films. He is currently in pre-production for his first feature film, *Meeting Ms. Leigh*. He graduated *cum laude* from Cleveland State University, where he also played Division I basketball. He won the Horizon League Sportsmanship Award in 2014.

Vince Font is an award-winning writer, book editor, and founder of Glass Spider Publishing. He is the author of the *Shadows on the Page* book series and the co-author of *American Sons: The Untold Story of the Falcon and the Snowman*.

About the Publisher

Glass Spider Publishing was founded in 2016 by writer Vince Font to help independent and self-published authors reach readers through professionally edited and artfully designed books. The company is headquartered in Ogden, Utah, but has published authors throughout world including the United States, Canada, the United Kingdom, and (as of this publication) Africa.

Made in the USA
Middletown, DE
28 October 2021

50534284R00061